Early Days with JESUS
AT THE ZOO

The Ross family

Nan Drew, Matthew, Mum, Dad, Gran Ross, Grandpa Ross

Shags, Ben, Kate, Sparks

Published and produced by CWR, Waverley Abbey House, Waverley Lane, Farnham, Surrey GU9 8EP
Writer: Jenny King; Drawings: Harold King Typeset by Watermark, Honing, Norfolk
Printed by Crusade Printing, Hampshire   ISBN 1-85345-048-0
© CWR 1991 All rights reserved. No part of this publication may be reproduced without the prior permission in writing of CWR
Reprinted 1996 All Scripture quotations are from the Good News Bible Copyright © American Bible Society, New York 1976

NATIONAL DISTRIBUTORS
AUSTRALIA Christian Marketing Pty Ltd., PO Box 519, Belmont, Victoria 3216 Tel: (052) 413 288
CANADA CMC Distribution Ltd., PO Box 7000, Niagara on the Lake, Ontario LOS 1JO Tel: 1-800-325-1297
MALAYSIA Salvation Book Centre (M), 23 Jalan SS2/64, Sea Park, 47300 Petaling Jaya, Selangor Tel: (3) 7766411
NEW ZEALAND Christian Marketing NZ Ltd., Private Bag, Havelock North Tel: 0508 535659 (toll free)
NIGERIA FBFM, (Every Day with Jesus), Prince's Court, 37, Ahmed Onibudo Street, Victoria Island Tel: 2611365, 866451, 613836
REPUBLIC OF IRELAND Scripture Union, 40 Talbot Street, Dublin 1 Tel: (01) 8363764
SINGAPORE Campus Crusade Asia Ltd 315 Outram Road 06-08 Tan Boon Liat Building Singapore 169074 Tel: (65) 2223640
SOUTH AFRICA Struik Christian Books (Pty Ltd) PO Box 193, Maitland 7405 Cape Town Tel: (021) 551 5900
USA CMC Distribution, P.O. Box 644, Lewiston, New York, 14092-0644 Tel: 1-800-325-1297

How to use Early Days

Early Days has been designed to help parents to teach simple Bible truths in an exciting and practical way.

Choose a quiet area to work and have the materials (if any) needed for the activity at hand. You will find it most helpful to use the Good News Bible as this is the version that the *Early Days* notes are based upon.

Read the Bible verse and then the story, and try to involve your child as much as possible. Encourage him/her to talk about the reading and the story and add your own comments. Try to help your child understand the theme.

Take time to do the activity for the day, but don't worry if you can't finish it or if you miss a few days. It's better to "get together" every other day for a longer time than to rush every day.

After you have completed the activity, say the prayer at the bottom of the page. Encourage your child to add to this prayer time, perhaps including people or situations that you think are relevant.

Harold and Jenny King

📖 = Bible reading   🙏 = Prayer

📖 Revelation 4:11

Everyone was in a rush. Dad was late for work and he had to take Matthew to Nan's on the way. Mum was making the breakfast, packing a picnic and trying to do Kate's hair. They were dropping Kate at playgroup on the way to Ben's school. His class was going to the zoo and Mum was coming too!

Draw your favourite picnic foods.

Dear Jesus, please let me be helpful when everyone is in a rush.

Job 38:14

At last it was time to leave. Mrs Court, Ben's teacher, had checked the register and everyone climbed onto the bus. Ben stared out of the window as they passed houses, shops and factories, then fields, trees and farms. Suddenly the bus stopped and they were there! Out piled everyone, two by two, "Just like the animals going into the ark," thought Ben.

Cut slots and pull strip through.
See last page for strip.

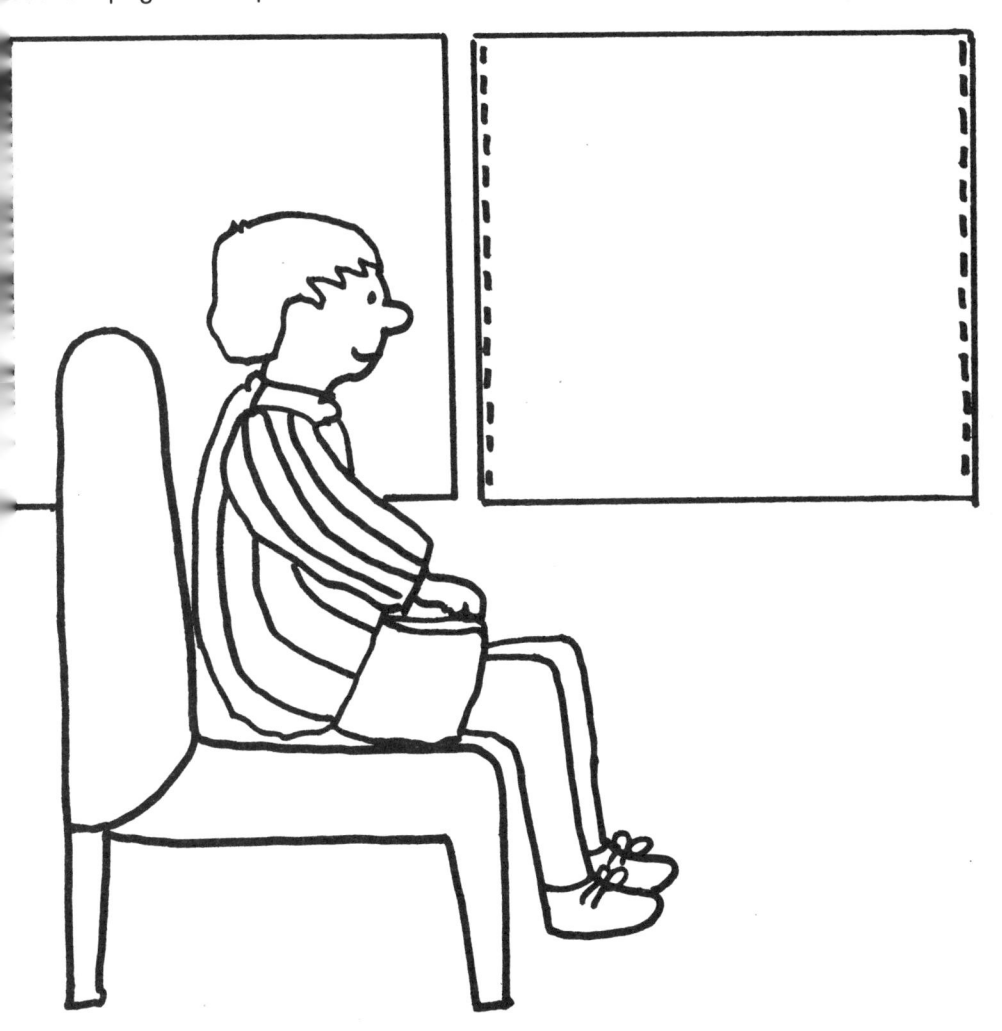

Thank You, God, for the countryside.

Gen 7:1, 8a, 9

"The Lord said to Noah, 'Go into the boat with your whole family; I have found that you are the only one in all the world who does what is right.' A male and a female of every kind of animal and bird went into the boat with Noah, as God had commanded."

Colour in.

Dear Jesus, please help me to be obedient.

📖 Gen 7:10, 17, 18, 22

"Seven days later the flood came. The flood continued for forty days, and the water became deep enough for the boat to float. The water became deeper, and the boat drifted on the surface. Everything on earth that breathed died."

Colour in.

Dear Jesus, please take care of people when there are floods.

Gen 8:1, 4, 6–7

"God had not forgotten Noah and all the animals with him in the boat; he caused a wind to blow, and the water started going down. On the seventeenth day of the seventh month the boat came to rest on a mountain in the Ararat range. After forty days Noah opened a window and sent out a raven. It did not come back, but kept flying around until the water was completely gone."

Colour in.

Dear Jesus, please take care of people who travel by boat.

Gen 8:8–11

"Meanwhile, Noah sent out a dove to see if the water had gone down, but since the water still covered all the land, the dove did not find a place to alight. It flew back to the boat, and Noah reached out and took it in. He waited another seven days and sent out the dove again. It returned to him in the evening with a fresh olive leaf in its beak. So Noah knew that the water had gone down."

Colour in.

Thank You, God, for beautiful birds.

📖 Gen 8:18–19

"So Noah went out of the boat with his wife, his sons, and their wives. All the animals and birds went out of the boat in groups of their own kind."

Colour in.

🙏 Thank You, God, that You always take care of me.

📖 Gen 1:24

Once through the gates the class split into groups. There was so much to look at, all those animals — monkeys swinging from branch to branch, giraffes with long necks, lions with fluffy manes and, of course, the elephants with their long trunks.

Colour in shapes with dots to find the animal.

Thank You, God, for making all the animals.

📖 Gen 1:20–22

Next came the birds, brightly coloured parrots, tiny finches, toucans with their strange beaks and peacocks with their beautiful tails.

Finger paint or draw the peacock tail.

🙏 Thank You, God, for all You have made.

📖 Psalm 104:24–25

At 11 o'clock all the groups met up to go into the aquarium. Inside, they saw so many fish, all different shapes and sizes and, as well, there were starfish, crabs, sea horses, and even a huge octopus with lots of legs.

Stick on silver paper and scraps. Cover with cellophane.

🙏 Thank You, God, for fish and everything that lives in the water.

📖 Proverbs 30:24–28

After the fish was the insect house. Some of the girls were scared and Mum Ross wasn't very keen. Even though she knew God had made them, Mum didn't like things with lots of legs that scuttled about, especially spiders, so she offered to walk the girls around the pond instead.

Make a pipe cleaner spider.
Bind with wool or string to make body.

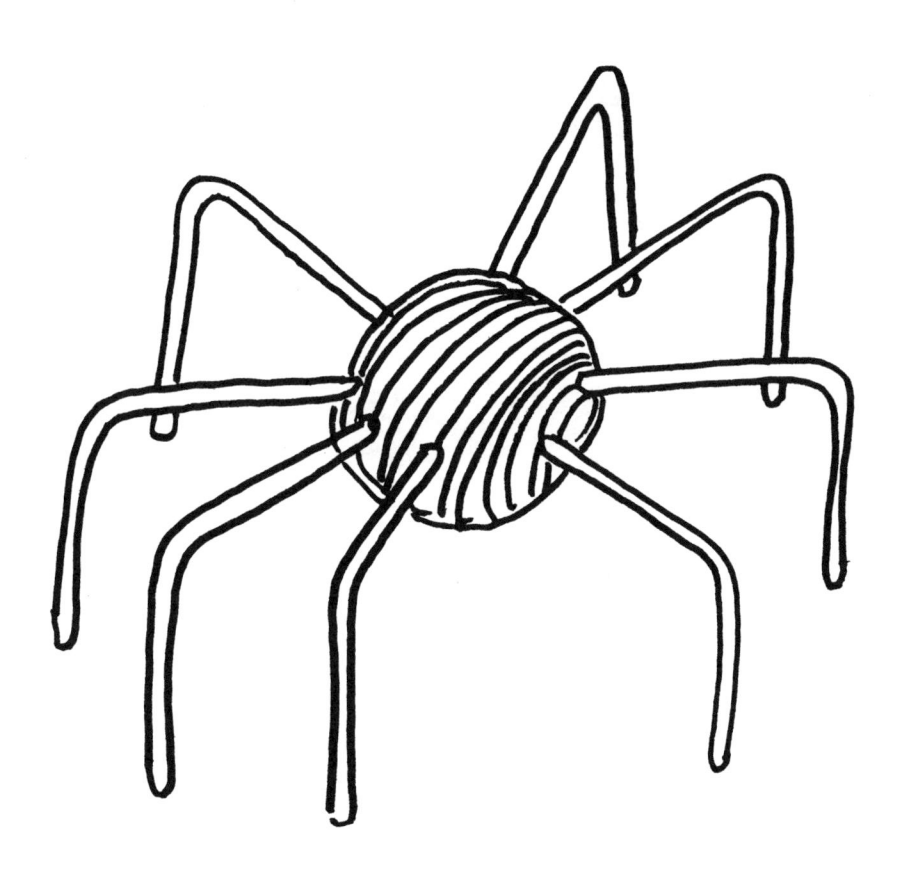

🙏 Dear Jesus, please take care of me when I'm scared.

📖 Job 37:5, 38:39–41, 39:13, 17–18, 26–28

Ben enjoyed the insects though, especially the huge butterflies and the bees inside their hive making a comb.

Make a butterfly by folding a piece of paper in half. Paint on one half and when still wet re-fold and press to make whole butterfly.

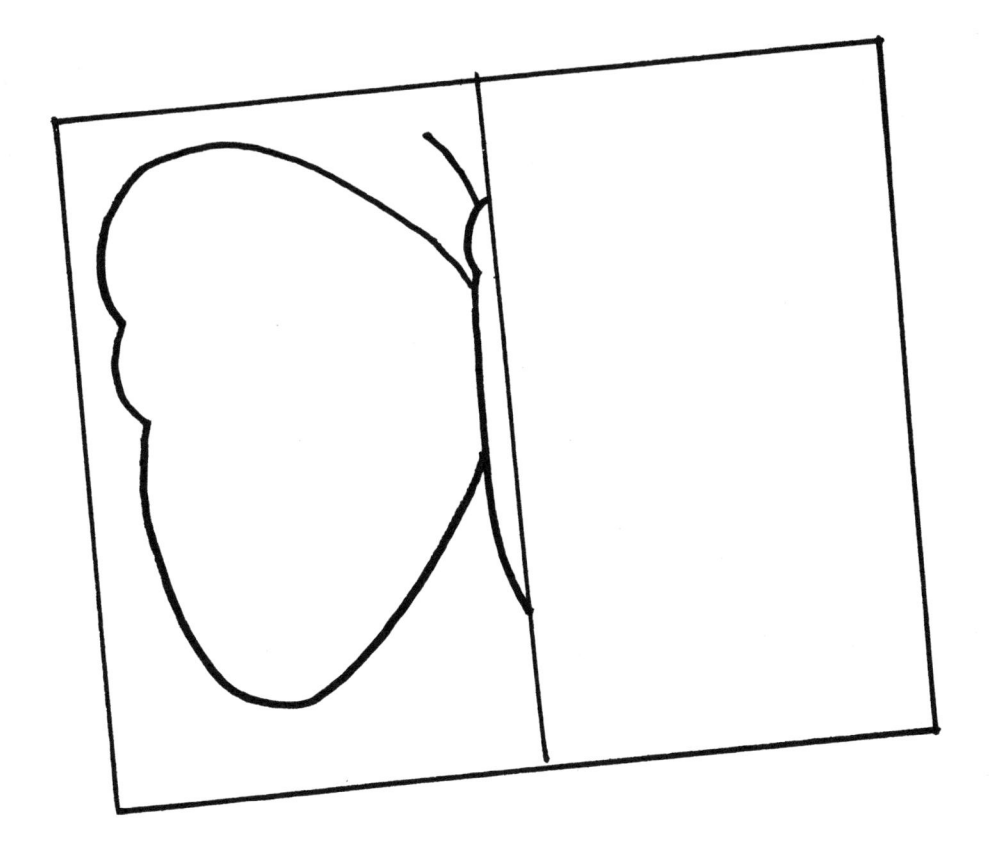

Thank You, God, for all Your creatures.

📖 Job 40:15–24

Just before lunch came the reptile house. Now it was Ben's turn to be worried. He wasn't sure about the slithering, slimy ones. But it was all right, everything was behind glass. There were even baby crocodiles, as well as snakes, frogs, turtles and lizards.

Make a frog.
Cut paper strip for body and narrow
strips for arms. Fold and glue on arms.

Stick on eyes. Use card for feet.
See last page for eyes and template for feet.

Dear Jesus, please help me to be brave.

📖 Psalm 104:24, 27–28

At last it was lunchtime. Mum's group, including Ben, decided to eat in the Pets' corner. As they ate, they watched the keeper taking care of the animals. He cleaned out the rabbits' and guinea pigs' enclosure just like Ben's class had to clean the cages at school. Then he gave them fresh cabbage and carrots too.

Cut out to make a jigsaw.

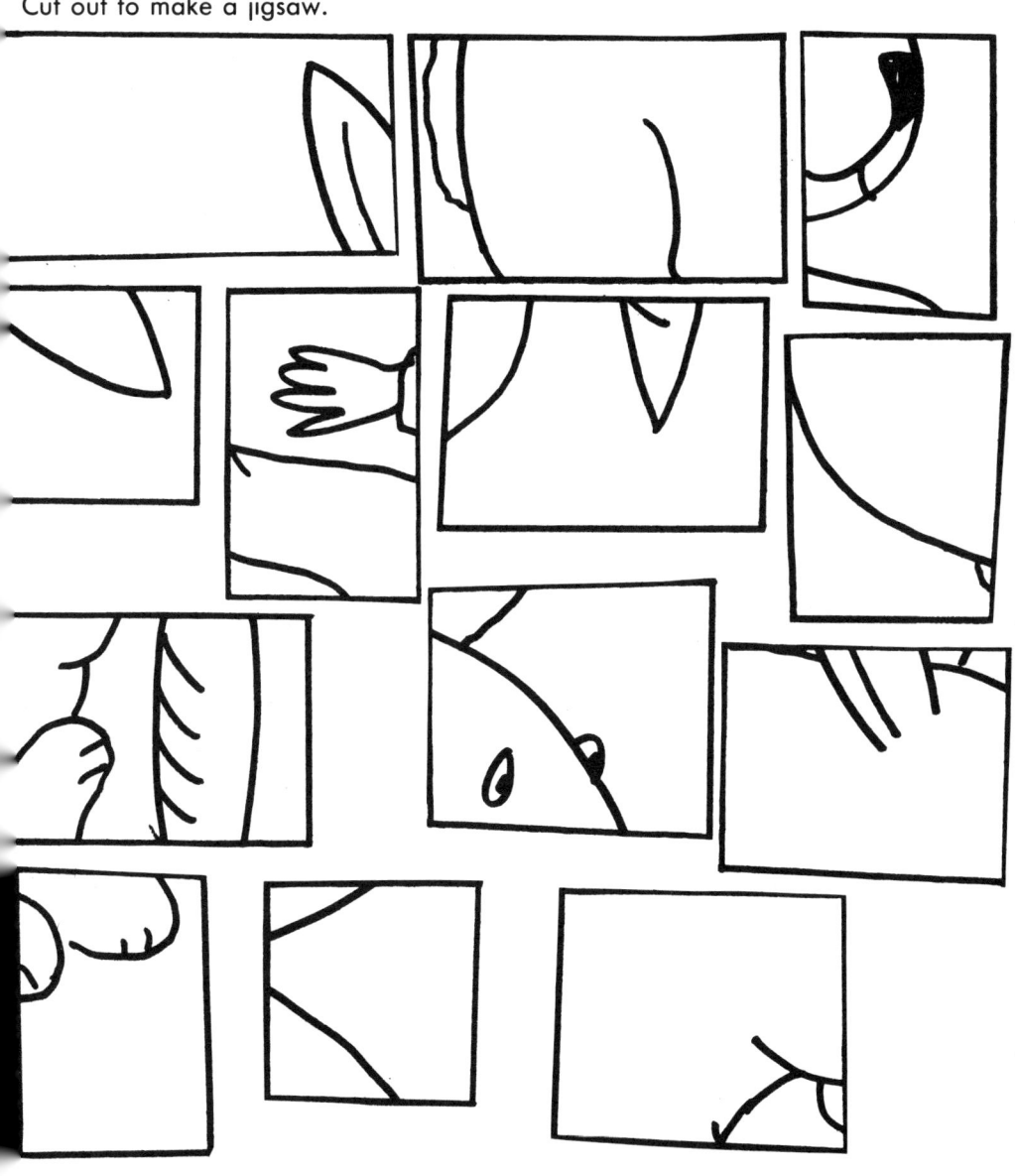

Thank You, God, for pets.

📖 Psalm 104:10–12

Another keeper was cleaning the aviary. There were feathers everywhere, then she replaced the water and filled up the seed exactly the way Ben did for his bird Sparks at home.

Find six differences in these pictures.

🙏 Dear God, please help people who care for birds and for animals.

📖 Luke 12:6–7

When they had all finished eating Ben tipped his crumbs down for the sparrows. Mum collected all her group together and led them to the place where they would meet the others.

Draw a line to the same birds.

Dear Jesus, please help me to take care of my pets.

📖 John 10:2–4

"The man who goes in through the gate is the shepherd of the sheep. The gatekeeper opens the gate for him; the sheep hear his voice as he calls his own sheep by name, and he leads them out. When he has brought them out, he goes ahead of them, and the sheep follow him, because they know his voice."

Colour in.

Dear Jesus, please help me to follow You.

📖 John 10:11–15

"I am the good shepherd, who is willing to die for the sheep. When the hired man, who is not a shepherd and does not own the sheep, sees a wolf coming, he leaves the sheep and runs away; so the wolf snatches the sheep and scatters them. The hired man runs away because he is only a hired man and does not care about the sheep. I am the good shepherd. As the Father knows me and I know the Father, in the same way I know my sheep and they know me. And I am willing to die for them."

Colour in.

Dear Lord, I'm glad You know me.

📖 Matthew 6:26

Just as Mum's group met up with the class, Mrs Squires, Ben's dinner lady, rushed up. One of her group was missing. Alan Greig had just disappeared.

Help Mrs. Squire to find Andrew.

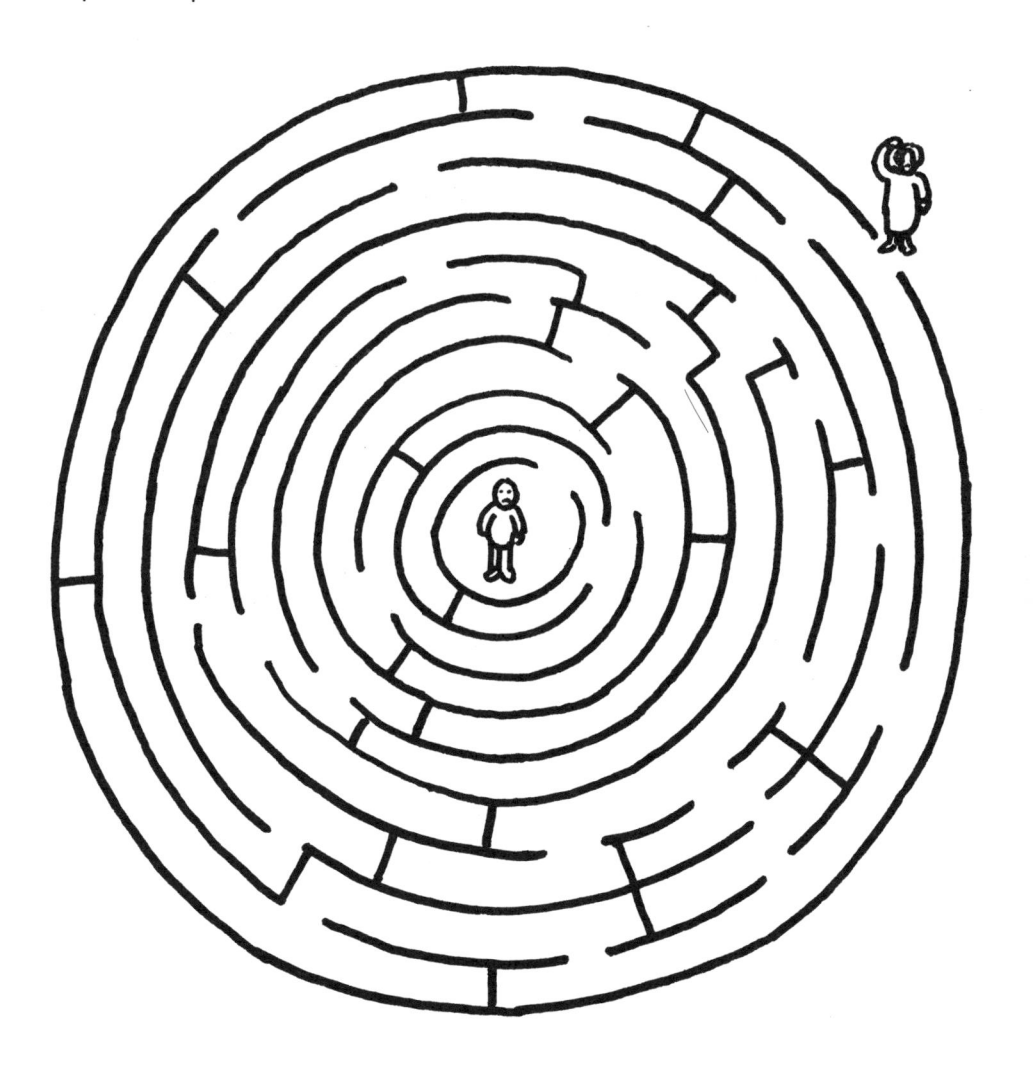

🙏 Dear Jesus, please take care of people who are lost and alone.

📖 Psalm 94:19.

Mrs Court told all the class to sit down on the grass while she sent two of the mums off with Mrs Squires to search. Mrs Court looked very worried, but a bit cross too.

Draw a line to put the right animal in right house.

Dear Jesus, help me to do as I am told.

📖 Luke 15:4–6

"Suppose one of you has a hundred sheep and loses one of them — what does he do? He leaves the other ninety-nine sheep in the pasture and goes looking for the one that got lost until he finds it. When he finds it, he is so happy that he puts it on his shoulders and carries it back home. Then he calls his friends and neighbours together and says to them, 'I am so happy I found my lost sheep. Let us celebrate!'"

Colour in.

Dear Jesus, thank You for always watching over me.

📖 Psalm 89:1–2

Soon they were back and Alan was with them. He had been crying. He'd wandered off to look at the bears and then couldn't find the others. Mrs Court took Alan to one side, spoke to him firmly, then smiled, gave him a hug and turned back to the class – "Come on everyone, we're off to meet the keeper."

Make a bear out of a brown paper bag.
Stuff the bag with paper, seal end with sticky tape.
Draw on a face. Cut out and stick on
ears. Use paper for legs.

Dear Jesus, thank You that You always forgive me.

📖 Psalm 8:4–9

The children all followed Mrs Court into a big hut. It was quite dark inside. There were pictures and maps on the walls, and some boxes covered with cloths. Everyone was very quiet.

Draw from dot to dot to find animal.

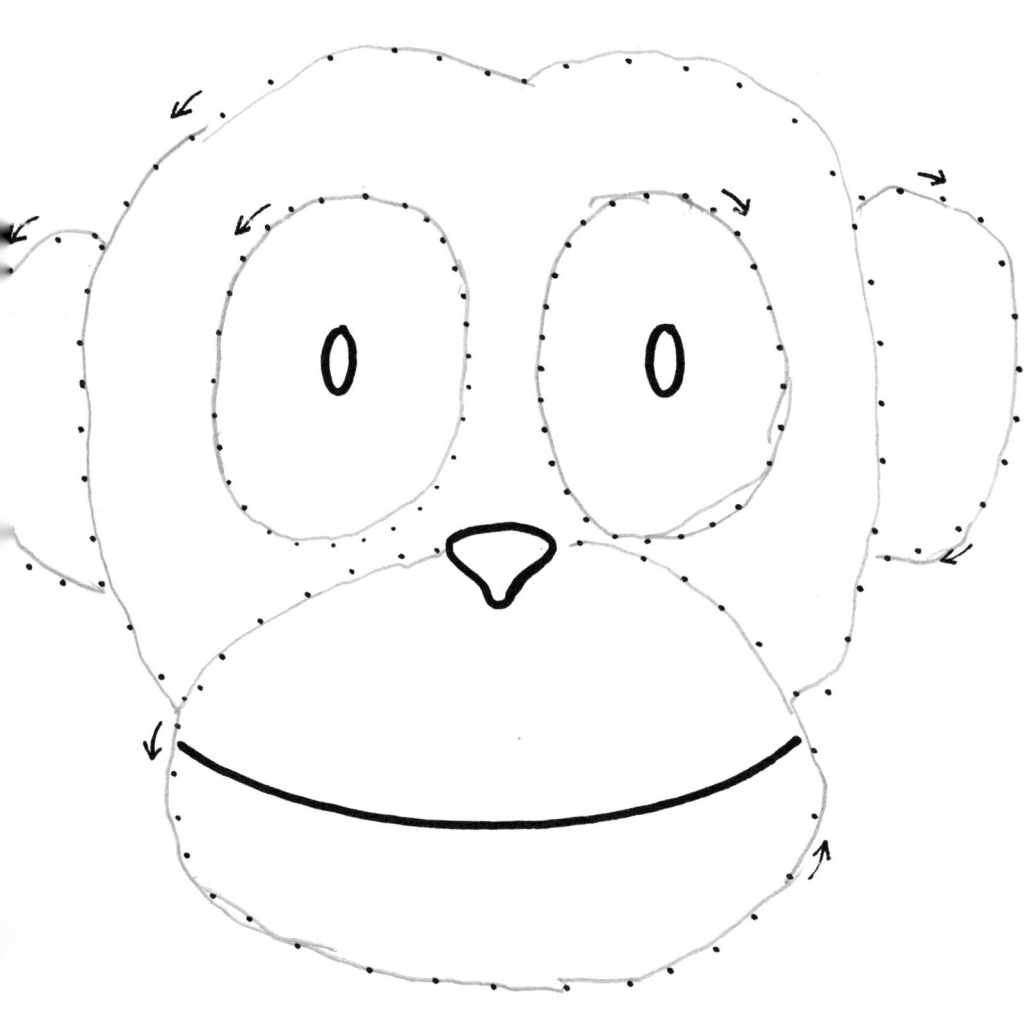

Thank You, God, for quiet times.

Psalm 36:7–8

Mr Bryant, the keeper, welcomed everyone to the zoo. Then he asked the children why they thought the animals were there. Ben put up his hand quickly, so did lots of the others. Everyone had the same answer — for people to come and look at them. Yes ....

aw your favourite bird.

Thank You, God, for all the people who take care of animals.

📖 Genesis 1:27–31

Mr Bryant went on to tell the children there were other reasons for zoos too. In some countries there are not many wild animals left, so they need protecting and taking care of. Ben remembered Uncle Jack telling him that in Africa lots of elephants are killed so that their ivory tusks can be sold to carve.

Make a 3D animal.

Fold a sheet of card in half. Draw on animal, colour in and cut out.

🙏 Dear Jesus, forgive us for being greedy.

📖 Psalm 148:9–10

Mr Bryant then lifted off one of the cloths. Underneath was a red and blue parrot in a cage. In South America, he told the children, the forests are being cut down for roads and farming so there is nowhere for the parrots to live.

Stick on scraps or coloured paper.

Dear Jesus, please let all the world care about our animals and birds.

📖 Psalm 104:16–17

On the wall was a picture of some pandas eating bamboo. Mr Bryant showed the class on a map of China that there is not so much bamboo grown now.

Stick on drinking straws or tissue for bamboo.

🖋 Dear Jesus, please let animals have enough to eat.

📖 Psalm 36:5–6

Last of all, Mr Bryant lifted another cloth, put his hand in a tank and lifted out a snake. Ben moved closer to Mum. The keeper explained that snakes weren't really slimy and they are often killed so their skins can be used for shoes and handbags. Then Mr Bryant said goodbye and invited the children to stroke the snake, now hanging around his neck, as they went out. Ben did, he was surprised – it wasn't slimy at all!

Make a bouncy snake.

Draw a snake shape onto a piece of paper, colour in, cut out.

Thank You, God, for surprises.

📖 Psalm 69:34

On the way back to the bus there was just enough time to watch the penguins and seals being fed. They were so funny — the way they walked and then dived under the water after the fish.

Make a toilet roll penguin. See last page for beak, etc.

🖊 Thank You, God, for fun.

📖 Psalm 50:10–11

Back in the coach, Ben felt very tired. He had so much to remember to tell Dad and Nan, Kate and Matthew. All those different animals that God had made. Soon Ben was asleep against Mum's arm, dreaming of elephants, frogs, parrots, rabbits, monkeys and lots more too.

Find four animals and two birds in this picture.

🙏 Thank You, God, for Your wonderful world.

Penguin

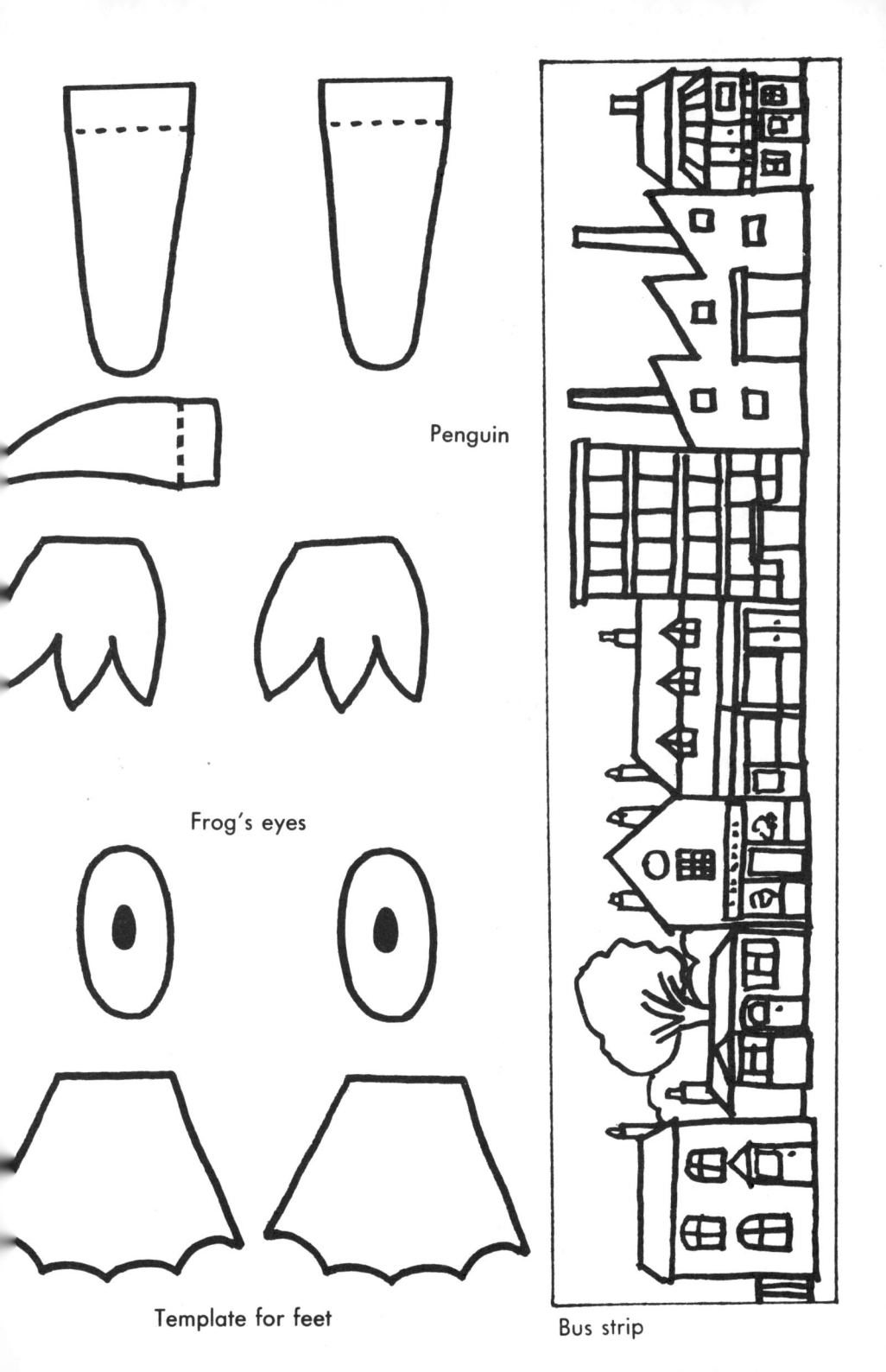

Frog's eyes

Template for feet

Bus strip

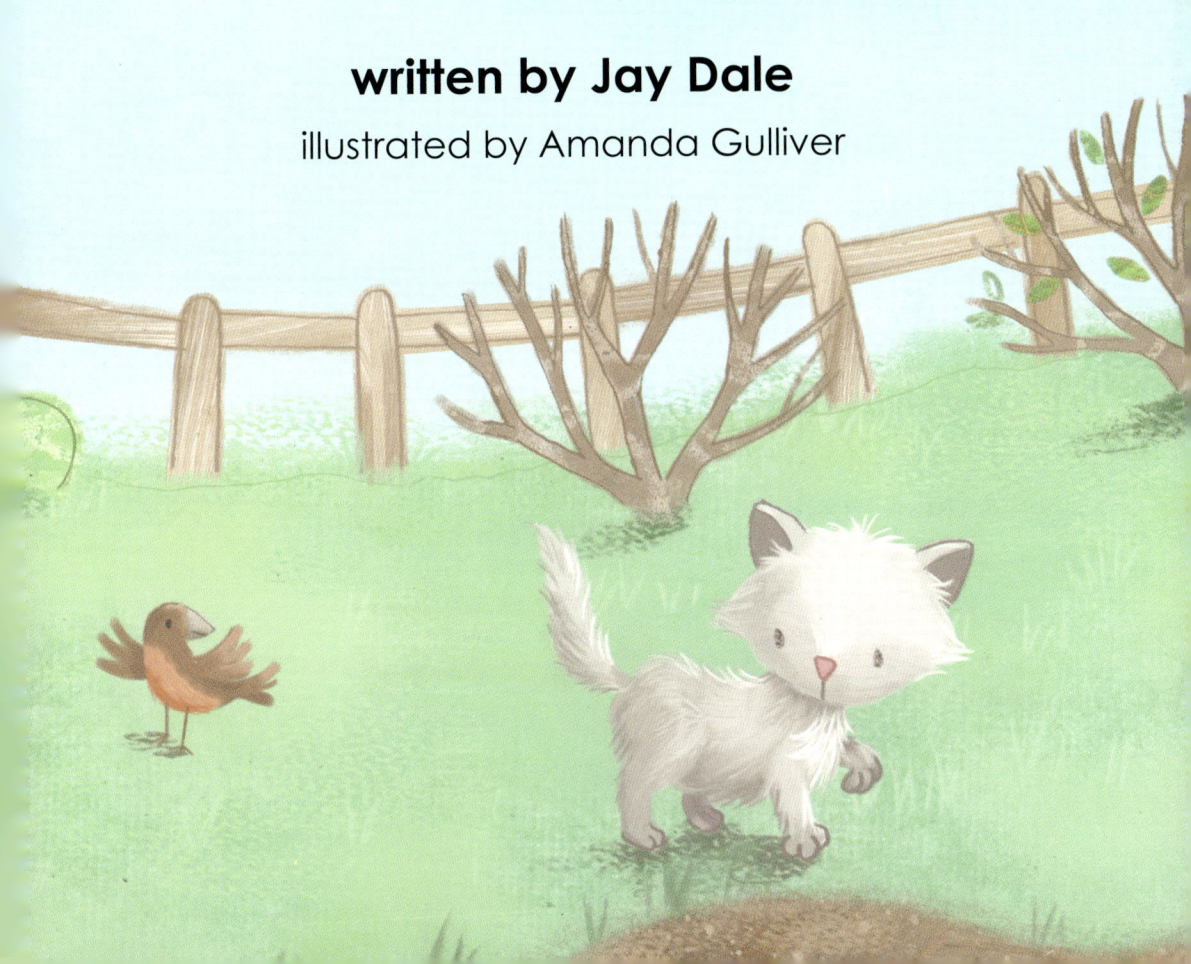

Lea and Dad Make a Garden

written by Jay Dale

illustrated by Amanda Gulliver

"Dad," said Lea.
"Can we make
a garden today?
I can see 4 little pots.
I can see 4 little plants too!"

3

"Look!" said Dad.
"We can make
a garden today."

"It is fun to make
a garden!"
said Lea.

5

"Come with me," said Dad.

Dad and Lea went inside the shed.

"Look!" said Dad.

"Oh," said Lea.
"I can make the garden with you."

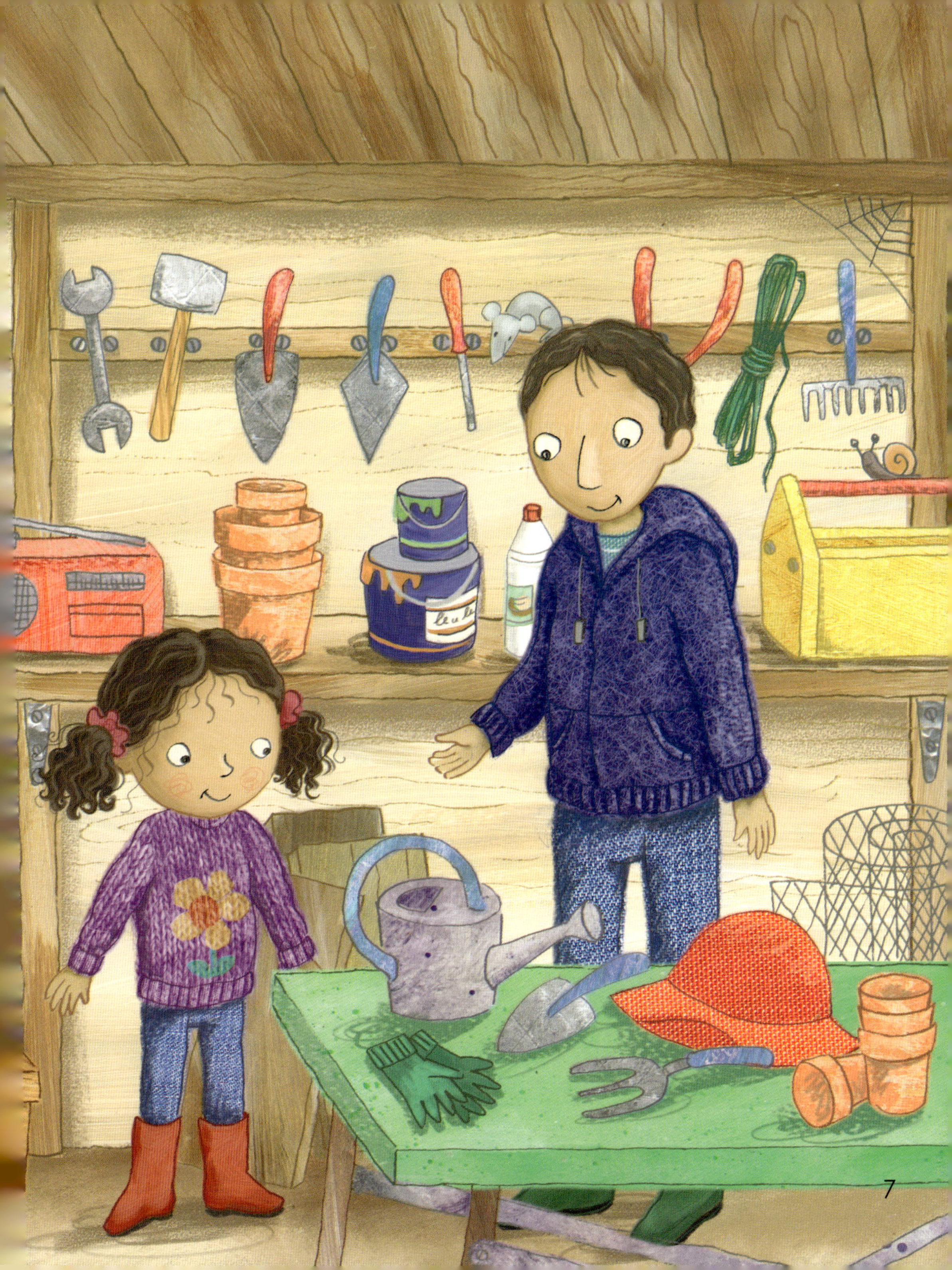

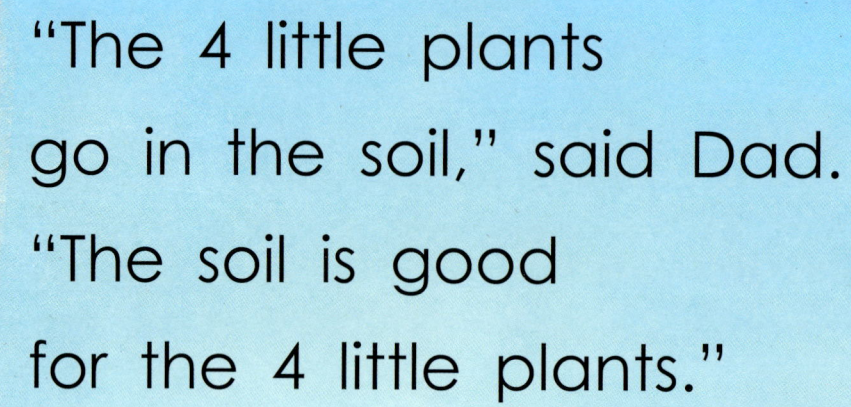

"The 4 little plants go in the soil," said Dad. "The soil is good for the 4 little plants."

9

"This is fun!" said Lea.
"I like looking after the 4 little plants."

bean tomato bean tomato

11

"Dad!" shouted Lea.
"Come and look
at the 4 little plants."

13

"Look!" said Lea.
"The 4 little plants are big."

"Oh!" said Dad.
"The 4 little plants **are** big!"

tomato

"I like this garden,"
said Lea.

"I like it too," said Dad.